The Birthday Book

Bonus

HOW TO MAKE A
BIRTHDAY TIME CAPSULE!

by **Tina Forrester** and **Sheryl Shapiro**
art by **Suzane Langlois**

Annick Press
Toronto ≈ New York ≈ Vancouver

contents

Happy

Birthday

Icing on the cake

Special days like birthdays are rare, aren't they? You probably wish there were more of them. One way to relive the fun is to save mementos. Imagine how wonderful you'll feel when you rediscover the keepsakes!

Looking at, touching, sniffing, or listening to whatever you have put away will bring back warm memories, maybe even make a rainy day feel sunny.

Throughout this book are cool suggestions of souvenirs you might like to keep. Then at the back of the book, there are ways to pack your treasures in a simple time capsule.

Have a GREAT day— one you'll remember for a long time!

Let's Party

Cakes, candles, and birthdays go together, a tradition that began thousands of years ago.

Ancient Greeks who worshiped the moon goddess took round cakes—shaped like a full moon—to her temple on her special day. To make the cakes glow like the moon, they added lighted candles.

So, why do we blow our birthday candles out?

Long ago, people believed that one day a year—the anniversary of the day they were born—evil spirits could work wicked charms on them. To warn the spirits off, they proved they were way too powerful to harm by blowing all their candles out with one deep breath.

To further defend birthday celebrants, friends and family got together to guard them with good thoughts, best wishes, and gifts—the first birthday parties!

Hmmm ... a cake with candles? It must be someone's birthday! You can't put the cake in your time capsule, but you can save the candles!

In olden times, only kings were important enough to have birthday parties. This might be why today some boys and girls wear paper crowns at their celebration.

In China, birthday kids celebrate by eating the longest possible noodles, symbols of a very long life.

Keep this, toss that—choosing treasures, what a pleasure!

Time Capsule Ideas

- A party invitation
- Some birthday cards
- Wrapping paper and ribbons
- Your birthday menu
- Party napkins
- List of gifts
- Candles from your cake
- Party decorations
- Photos of your party
- Guest list

Beside each dot is an example of an artifact or a bit of information you might like to include in your time capsule. The examples are only suggestions. You can probably think of many more. You decide what mementos you keep.

That's the Spirit

Friends and families everywhere love thinking of ways to join in the birthday fun.

Would you believe that some American and Canadian kids start their big day by waking up to a kind-hearted pinch meant to ensure good luck? Others open their sleepy eyes to see a room filled with bouncing balloons, or a doorway decorated with colorful streamers, one for each year. But imagine awakening to a giggling sister or brother smearing a dab of butter on your nose! In Newfoundland it's a birthday custom that's supposed to help smooth the way for the coming year.

For many families, breakfast in bed is a birthday tradition—an awesome tray filled with delicious goodies. But some families like to include friends in the fun, so they "kidnap" the birthday person's best buddy and everyone eats breakfast at a local restaurant still wearing their pajamas!

Another common family custom is to serve a special birthday lunch or dinner, but some families make it uncommon by eating the meal backwards. Yep: dessert first! What a treat, don't you think?

How much have you grown this year? Many families measure their kids' heights on their birthdays!

What do you get if you cross an Elephant with a Kangaroo? Big holes all over Australia.

Many Danish families announce that someone inside their house is a year older by flying a flag outside a window.

In Holland, some families decorate the birthday person's dining-room chair with flowers, paper streamers, or balloons.

If a friend or family member in Argentina gently pulls eight times on someone's earlobe, it means ... happy eighth birthday!

Keep this, toss that—choosing treasures, what a pleasure!

Time Capsule Ideas

- Sketch of your family tree
- Cartoon of your family's birthday traditions
- Photos of your family and friends
- A copy of your birth certificate
- Cards sent from far away
- Names of your best friends, especially the ones you like to share popcorn with!
- Your height on your birthday

How Sweet It Is!

Think about cold, creamy ice cream melting on your tongue. Mmm, good! Was vanilla the flavor you imagined? Today, many kids like vanilla best, but when Europeans first tried vanilla, it was always mixed with chocolate. More than half a century later, an apothecary (something like a pharmacist) decided vanilla made a neat flavoring on its own.

Speaking of chocolate, the first was quite bitter. Many people who sampled it turned their noses up … until someone thought to add sugar. Now chocolate is another North American favorite.

Kids in other parts of the world often have favorite ice cream flavors that most Americans and Canadians have never even tried. Filipinos might choose ube, which is flavored with purple yams. Jamaicans might select soursop, a fruit with spiky green skin and a sweet-sour taste. And many Japanese love adzuki bean—small, reddish-brown beans that have a strong nutty-sweet taste.

The flavors of your birthday treats often depend on where you live and what you're used to.

Roasted spiders, anyone? The Piaroa of Venezuela think this exotic treat, which tastes something like shrimp or crab, is the perfect treat to offer visitors.

Tibetans, Mongolians, and people in parts of western China put salt in their tea instead of sugar.

How about some raw sugar cane? Kids who live in warm climates enjoy chewing this crunchy, juicy, giant grass from which our table sugar comes.

Keep this, toss that—choosing treasures, what a pleasure!

Time Capsule Ideas

- Magazine clippings of the foods you like best
- Photo of birthday cake
- Best frosting flavor
- Great jelly bean flavors
- List of excellent pizza toppings
- Best ice cream flavor
- Yuckiest food ever!
- List all your party foods
- Delicious family dessert recipe

Which candles burn longer, those on a boy's birthday cake or those on a girl's? Neither! Candles always burn shorter.

Beside each dot is an example of an artifact or a bit of information you might like to include in your time capsule. The examples are only suggestions. You can probably think of many more. You decide what mementos you keep.

Same Game
Different Name

Pin the __ on the __? Hmm. You probably think this game is Pin the Tail on the Donkey—but it doesn't have to be! At your birthday party you can play something a little different, like Pin the Nose on the Clown or Pin the Spaceship in Outer Space.

You can also adapt the old memory game in which the first player says, "In my grandmother's trunk I found …" and names any item. The second player repeats what the first said and adds a second item, and so on. When a player misses an item, he's out. One way to change the game is to say, "At my birthday party I like to eat …" Just make sure the winner doesn't try to eat everything on the final list!

See if you recognize this game: Two Chinese children face each other and chant three times *ching, chang, pok* as they move their arms and fists up and down like hammers. On the last beat of the third round, they each reveal a fist closed like a stone, two fingers opened like scissors, or five fingers flat like paper. You guessed it! It's Stone, Scissors, Paper. Japanese boys and girls play it too, but call it *jan, ken, pon*.

Hooray for party games—fun, applause, prizes, and laughs.

Indonesians call jump rope *lompat tali*. And girls in China and Colombia play jump rope too, but instead of rope they use chain-linked rubber bands.

Gotcha! You're it! When you hear these words, do you freeze, go to jail, or try to catch someone else? Tag is a game played around the world. The rules may be different, but you'd probably recognize it. Tigged (tagged) English children playing Tiggy Off Ground are safe if their feet are, well, off the ground. In Pakistan, kids play *oonch neech*, and players are safe when they stand on something high.

Hopscotch, hide-and-seek, marbles, jacks, and checkers are other games kids play almost everywhere.

Keep this, toss that—choosing treasures, what a pleasure!

Time Capsule Ideas

- **Names of fun party games**
- **Pictures of the coolest teams**
- **Rookie cards**
- **Sports you like to play**
- **Ideas for your own game**
- **Sports posters**
- **Favorite sport to watch**
- **Coach's name**
- **Greatest video game ever**
- **Your highest scores**
- **Names of awesome board games**

What do you give a two-hundred-pound sumo wrestler for his birthday? Anything he wants!

Excellent Magic

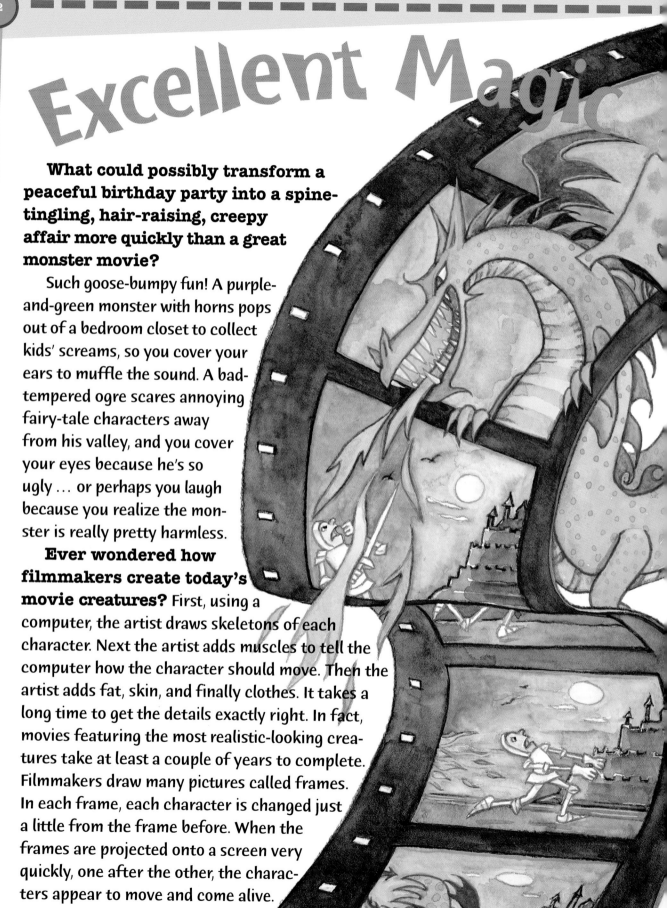

What could possibly transform a peaceful birthday party into a spine-tingling, hair-raising, creepy affair more quickly than a great monster movie?

Such goose-bumpy fun! A purple-and-green monster with horns pops out of a bedroom closet to collect kids' screams, so you cover your ears to muffle the sound. A bad-tempered ogre scares annoying fairy-tale characters away from his valley, and you cover your eyes because he's so ugly … or perhaps you laugh because you realize the monster is really pretty harmless.

Ever wondered how filmmakers create today's movie creatures? First, using a computer, the artist draws skeletons of each character. Next the artist adds muscles to tell the computer how the character should move. Then the artist adds fat, skin, and finally clothes. It takes a long time to get the details exactly right. In fact, movies featuring the most realistic-looking creatures take at least a couple of years to complete. Filmmakers draw many pictures called frames. In each frame, each character is changed just a little from the frame before. When the frames are projected onto a screen very quickly, one after the other, the characters appear to move and come alive.

Blankets, pillows, popcorn, a great video: a sleepover birthday!

When you watch five hours of TV, you see at least one hour of commercials.

Do you know where a cow goes on its birthday?   To the mooooovies!

Walt Disney created the world's first animated cartoons, but they weren't meant for kids. They were two-minute advertising films shown at movie theaters.

Keep this, toss that—choosing treasures, what a pleasure!

Time Capsule Ideas

- Titles of awesome TV shows
- Coolest cartoon character
- Number of hours you watch TV each week
- Copy of your best joke
- Movie ticket stub
- Photo of a favorite movie star
- Name of the funniest movie you've seen
- The kind of movie you love to watch
- Description of excellent commercial

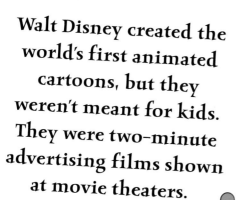

Wouldn't it be fun to make a home video of your birthday party to keep inside your time capsule?

Beside each dot is an example of an artifact or a bit of information you might like to include in your time capsule. The examples are only suggestions. You can probably think of many more. You decide what mementos you keep.

Brain Dancing

A pile of paper here ... a few books there ... a drawer full of pencils, pens, and crayons. Nowadays, lots of people just scatter writing and drawing materials throughout their home. But centuries ago, pens, ink, and paper were precious. Scribes had to print entire books by hand using homemade pens and ink. Each pen was really a feather: its shaft was slit, then cut on an angle to create a sharp point. Ink was made from berries, bark, or soot.

Instead of paper, scribes wrote on thin, dried animal skins called parchment and vellum. A scribe had to dip his pen into ink after every word or two. How frustrating if he pressed too hard! Too much pressure was sure to ruin the pen or leave an ugly blob of ink.

Crayons? The first ones—used to mark crates and barrels—were black, black, and, er, black. No colors! Imagine being the first birthday kid, approximately a century ago, to open a box of colorful crayons. It must have been pure magic.

Today our brains can dance with joy because we have so many materials—such as colored pencils, paint, stickers, glues, and even computers—to use.

Decorate invitations, dream up a dance,
or write a song—a creative birthday is cool!

What's the most frequently sung song in English? According to Guinness World Records, it's "Happy Birthday to You."

Did you know that a schoolteacher, Mildred Hill, wrote the melody and a principal, Dr. Patty Smith Hill, wrote the words to "Happy Birthday to You"? True!

They were sisters who worked in the same school in Louisville, Kentucky. They published the song more than a hundred years ago, in 1883.

An ordinary pencil can write 45,000 words or draw a line 56 km (35 miles) long.

Keep this, toss that—choosing treasures, what a pleasure!

Time Capsule Ideas

- Name of favorite book
- A poem or story you wrote this year
- Wrapping-paper collage
- Pictures you have drawn
- The color of your bedroom
- Photocopy of a great CD cover
- Lyrics of an awesome song
- Pictures of a singer you like
- Instrument you play
- A great riddle

Beside each dot is an example of an artifact or a bit of information you might like to include in your time capsule. The examples are only suggestions. You can probably think of many more. You decide what mementos you keep.

Chalk Talk

Your school is a place where lots of kids are turning the same age as you this year. And some of them are your friends. You go to their parties and they attend yours. But what if on school days, instead of hopping on a bus or walking with your friends, you stayed at home to learn? What do you think your days would be like?

Kids who attend "school" at home are called home-schoolers, and their moms or dads are their teachers. Most study math, reading, spelling, science ... all the things other kids learn. But some also spend many school hours on projects that suit their special interests, such as learning to play instruments, helping out at homeless shelters, and visiting museums and science centers.

Home-schoolers are rarely bored or lonely! They know lots of kids their own age. Besides learning and playing with other home-schoolers, they also play with kids who attend regular schools, and they often join groups like Scouts, community bands, and sports teams.

School buildings aren't the only places to meet other kids and "go to school."

How do you make seven an even number? Take the "s" off.

**This year, is your birthday on a school day?
Cupcakes for everyone!**

The school year for most kids in the U.S. and Canada is 180 days. That sure is a lot of days. But wait! Look at how many days kids in other countries go to school:

* Russia: 210 days
* Israel: 215 days
* Japan: 243 days
* China: 251 days

Left to right? Right to left? Arabic and Hebrew are read from right to left, which seems backwards to us but is natural for Arabs and Israelis. And the Chinese write in columns from top to bottom, starting on the right.

Keep this, toss that—choosing treasures, what a pleasure!

Time Capsule Ideas

○ Class picture
○ Teacher's name and photo
○ Name of bus driver or crossing guard
○ Things from the class play or musical
○ Class-trip information
○ What you like most about school
○ Favorite subject or project
○ Special classroom jobs
○ Names of kids you sit next to
○ Report card

We're Outta Here!

Why not party in the wide-open spaces!
We live on a fabulous planet—so many places to celebrate birthdays: the local park, sun-drenched beaches, vacant lots, snowy fields, and ice-covered rinks ... Er, snow and ice? Sure, as long as you're dressed for the cold.

Nothing beats a beach or pool party, especially on a hot summer day. Unless, of course, it's a party with lots of space for a friendly game of soccer, or hiding places for playing hide-and-go-seek. Another idea is to plan an outdoor scavenger or treasure hunt—everyone's a winner for sure if the search includes litter that in the end is properly thrown away. Top the day off with a campfire and roast marshmallows on sticks, and if it's getting dark, tell scary stories— the scarier the better, some kids say.

There's no need to celebrate your birthday inside just because the temperature outside dips below freezing. Instead, bundle up and head for an outdoor skating rink. If there's snow, build a magnificent fort or sculpture. To help everyone stay toasty, you can serve hot chocolate. **Yum!**

A packet of seeds, a plastic pot, and some soil
are loot-bag treats that continue to grow.

Be sure to recycle any plastic soda-pop bottles from your party.
Some may be transformed into fleecy fabric used to make warm outerwear.

Why do birds fly south in the winter? Because it's too far to walk!

Keep this, toss that—choosing treasures, what a pleasure!

Time Capsule Ideas

- Pressed leaf or flower
- Beautiful feathers and shells
- Drawing of the view from your window
- Photos taken on vacation
- Picture of favorite animal
- Wildflower seeds
- Unusual pebbles and stones
- Photos of family pets
- Drawings of bugs seen in a local park

As you grow a year older, so does our planet. Scientists believe that Earth is about three to five billion years old. Every April 22 is Earth Day, and many Americans and Canadians celebrate by sharing ideas about how all of us can make our planet a better place to live.

Other special days

If you're like most kids, your birthday could be any time of year—depending on the day you were born. That is, unless you live in China. Everyone there celebrates on the same day: Chinese New Year. Since this always happens in late January or early February, everyone in China has a winter birthday! For the festivities, Chinese decorate their homes with red for happiness and gold for wealth. At midnight, they open their doors and windows to let the old year out and the new one in.

Looking for something to celebrate? A few holidays you may not know are Share A Smile Day (celebrated on March 1 in classrooms across North America), International Day of Peace (observed on September 21 by countries that belong to the United Nations), and World Hello Day (celebrated on November 21 by friendly people in 180 countries).

Is your birthday your favorite day of the whole year?
Will you remember what made it special?

Can April March? No, but August May.

One favorite holiday originated about two thousand years ago. Northern Europeans known as Celts believed the year had two seasons: winter, which started on November 1, and summer, which started on May 1. October 31 – our Halloween – was once their New Year's Eve!

The Pilgrims ate with spoons, knives, and fingers—no forks— at the first Thanksgiving, almost four centuries ago. To keep their hands clean during the three-day feast, they wiped them on large napkins hung over their shoulders.

Keep this, toss that—choosing treasures, what a pleasure!

Time Capsule Ideas

- ○ Holiday greeting cards
- ○ Date of your best friend's birthday
- ○ List of new things to try this year
- ○ Something that reminds you of your favorite holiday
- ○ Holiday foods you love
- ○ First line of a seasonal tune
- ○ Drawing of your favorite season
- ○ Best thing that happened last year
- ○ What you want to be when you grow up

Beside each dot is an example of an artifact or a bit of information you might like to include in your time capsule. The examples are only suggestions. You can probably think of many more. You decide what mementos you keep.

Saving your birthday memories in a time capsule

Collecting souvenirs is cool, but discovering them later is thrilling! Just think of how amazing it will be to look through your birthday treasures in a few months or years—such great memories. Keepsakes help you remember the fun you shared with your friends, the games you played, and … yum! … the treats you ate.

But to keep all this wonderful stuff from becoming wrinkled, dusty, or torn, you need to find a container. Hmmm, how to choose the best kind for you?

The EASY ANSWER for keeping memorabilia 5 or 10 years is to use almost any box or bag, as long as it's clean and dry. You can choose something as simple as a zippered plastic bag or a plastic container with a lid.

However, the FUN ANSWER is to choose something you can decorate, such as a manila envelope, paper bag with handles, or cardboard box. Transform it into something magical, magnificent, or beautiful (maybe all three!) using crayons, paints, colored paper, and—most appropriate of all—some of the birthday treasures you've collected, like tags, stickers, bits of wrapping paper, and snippets of ribbon.

Before putting your treasures away, be sure to add a tag or piece of paper with the year that you celebrated this birthday because, believe it or not, by the time you rediscover your goodies, you may have forgotten. Then place your keep-sakes in a safe spot.

Happy collecting and saving!

For the serious collector

If you are serious about keeping your time capsule for a very long time—say 15 years or more—read on. Remember: materials deteriorate at different rates, depending on the temperature, amount of light, and humidity where they are stored. Most time capsules are kept aboveground in dark, dry places, but the idea of burying a time capsule is intriguing! Finding an appropriate container can be a challenge, however. In addition to being leakproof, rustproof, opaque, and durable, the container must also be able to withstand changing temperatures. If you live in an area that experiences freeze/thaw conditions, a large jar (or bottle) with metal cap is not a good idea; over time the glass will crack and the metal cap will corrode.

Stainless steel, aluminum, and polypropylene containers (like the containers that hold eight pounds of margarine) are all good choices. A box made of acid-free cardboard is fine, too, as long as you keep your capsule in a dark, dry place in your home.

The best choice is a stainless steel container with a close-fitting lid that's welded shut or clamped down with wing nuts. Stainless steel containers are expensive and hard to find, however, so the next best choice is actually two plastic (polypropylene) containers, one of which is at least one inch (2.5 cm) larger all around than the other. You'll need an adult to help you with this: pour one inch (2.5 cm) of hot wax into the bottom of the larger container and let it cool. Place the smaller container (filled with this book and artifacts, sealed) on the wax. Pour more hot wax to fill the larger container, and let it cool. Seal the larger container and you're ready to bury your time capsule.

Be sure to select acid-free materials. Newspapers are printed on low-grade paper that turns yellow and becomes brittle after a few years. What's more, newspaper produces acidic fumes that can stain other paper and cause it to become brittle too. So, rather than save newspaper clippings, it's better to photocopy them, preferably on acid-free paper. If you want to label anything, use a pencil; ink fades.

Glue? Use pH neutral PVA (polyvinyl acetate). It won't turn yellow, become brittle, or discolor other surfaces. You can also use photo corners. Forget Cellophane tape! It dries out and leaves ugly marks.

Plastic bags made of polyethylene (such as sandwich or zippered bags) and food containers made of polypropylene (like margarine tubs) are fine for storing individual artifacts for a few years. Plastics keep out dust and moisture. But remember: if really long term storage is your plan, plastics have been around for less than 50 years, so no one knows how well they'll last for a hundred.

One plastic to avoid is PVC (polyvinyl chloride, such as food wrap). In two or three years, ink from printed items can migrate to PVC. Also, PVCs can leave an oily residue on any artifacts they touch. Other products to avoid are rubber bands, rubber cement, and plywood. They give off acidic fumes that may cause other items in your capsule to deteriorate. And metals corrode, so watch those paper clips! Store metal, such as coins, in plastic sandwich bags.

Want to save some photos? Black and white is better than color, because color fades faster. The amount of time it takes for color photos to fade depends on the temperature and amount of light where you keep them, but fading happens even in the dark. Store them between sheets of Mylar®, in acid-free glassine envelopes (the kind stamps are often kept in), or in acid-free paper envelopes.

And if you're planning to store computer disks, CDs, audiotapes, or videotapes, keep in mind that the equipment used to play them may not exist even a few years from now.

If you want to leave it for posterity—say, for a hundred years from now—you'll need special archival materials, which you can get by contacting a company such as Gaylord Brothers at 800/448-6160 (US) or 800/841-5854 (Canada). Another source is University Products at 413/532-3372 (US), 416/858-7888 (Eastern Canada), or 604/731-3439 (Western Canada).

And finally, one last bit of advice: seal your capsule on a dry day, as high humidity can quicken deterioration.

Annick Press Ltd.

We acknowledge the support of the Canada Council for the Arts, the Ontario Arts Council, the Government of Ontario through the Ontario Book Publishers Tax Credit program and the Ontario Book Initiative, and the Government of Canada through the Book Publishing Industry Development Program (BPIDP) for our publishing activities.

Cataloging in Publication

Forrester, Tina
        The birthday book / written by Tina Forrester and Sheryl Shapiro ; illustrated by Suzane Langlois.

ISBN 1-55037-829-5 (bound).–ISBN 1-55037-767-1 (pbk.)

1. Birthdays--Juvenile literature. I. Shapiro, Sheryl II. Langlois, Suzane III. Title.

GT2430.F67 2003   j394.2   C2003-900868-1

The art in this book was rendered in watercolor.

Distributed in Canada by: Published in the U.S.A. by Annick Press (U.S.) Ltd.
Firefly Books Ltd.   Distributed in the U.S.A. by:
3680 Victoria Park Avenue   Firefly Books (U.S.) Inc.
Willowdale, ON   P.O. Box 1338
M2H 3K1   Ellicott Station
                                     Buffalo, NY 14205

Manufactured in China.

Visit us at: www.annickpress.com

To Connor, who loves cake and ice cream, and promises to eat more vegetables after his next birthday.
        —T.F.

For my father, who has celebrated 85 birthdays.
        —S.S.

To Françoise, my mother.
        —S.L.

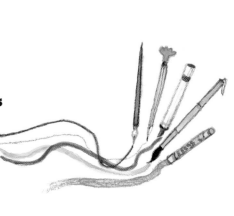

WITHDRAWN